Poems from the Heart

Annette Hoggs-Jackson

insight
PUBLISHING GROUP

Tulsa, Oklahoma

POEMS FROM THE HEART

© 2005 by Annette Hoggs-Jackson

Published by Insight Publishing Group
8801 S. Yale, Suite 410
Tulsa, OK 74137
918-493-1718

Unless otherwise noted, all Scripture quotations are taken from the King James Version of the Bible.

ISBN:1-932503-45-5
Library of Congress catalog card number: 2004115162

Printed in the United States of America

In Memory Of

Dorothy Mosley Hoggs
(A wonderful and loving mother)
I miss you

Thomas Hoggs Jr.
(Dad, thanks for being there and teaching me about life)
Dad, I love you much

Ministers
Thomas and Thelma Hoggs
(My grandparents)
who led me to Christ and gave me so much spiritual guidance. You were great teachers and left behind a great legacy. You showed me how to trust Him. He is the only way. One of my grandmother's favorite Scriptures is Mark 8:36, "For what shall it profit a man if he shall gain the whole world, and lose his own soul."

Dedication

This book is dedicated to my mother and father Thomas and Dorothy Hoggs. To my father Thomas Hoggs, with God anything is possible. And I give praise to God you are still around to see his miracles. To my husband, Sammy Jackson, who God sent to me through a prophecy. My husband is a man after God's own heart who believes God for the impossible. I love you very much. To my church family, Church of God Inc., and Pastor Fair and First Lady Grace Fair. I thank God for placing you in my path. To my son Tyrell Otaro, who is a blessing from God. To Samuel Jackson, my stepson, who loves God and basketball. To my immediate family, I love you much. To my only brother Thomas Hoggs III, we love you. To all my sisters, Sharon Hoggs-Hardy, Gina Hoggs, Barabara Hoggs-Abraham, Diane Hoggs, Carol Hoggs-Deburr, and Angela Hoggs. I am glad God has kept us all together.

Each one of you are very unique individuals. To my aunts and uncles who have been an inspiration to me: Alfred Mosley, Billy Mosley, Tina Hoggs, and Anna Hoggs. Apostle Sammy Hoggs and Bishop Curtis Hoggs, your faithfulness to God has taught me to be very committed to him. You have taught me how to love God. To all my nieces and nephews: Charles, Tamira, Brian, Brandon, April, Rashan, Vivian, Latoya, Jerry, Lisa, Devon, Jordan, Vanessa, Eugene, Ginea and Benjamin. Put God first in everything you do. To others who God spiritually placed in my path for a closer walk with him. May God continue to bless you.

Thanks for all the prayers that went forth for this book. Heavenly Father, most of all I give all praises to you. Thank you for placing this book and the words on my heart and for using me as your vessel to bring this book forth. Thank you for giving me a mission to write this book. I will continue to follow your plan for my life.

Contents

Acknowledgement

I would like to thank those who helped encourage me to write this book. I want to thank my family for being patient with me and for being understanding due to the long hours it took me to write this book. Thanks to my husband, Sammy Jackson, who told me that after submitting my work to others, I needed to write my own book. Thanks to Pastor Fair of Church of God Inc., in Lake Helen, Florida, who is my pastor and always offers words of encouragement. Thanks for guiding me spiritually and giving me words of encouragement. God has placed many spiritual people in my path to witness to others about God's love. Pastor Fair, you have also encouraged me to lead others to Christ. God used you as a vessel to give me a prophetic word as confirmation to write this book. Deborah Poole was also used by God as a vessel to give me a prophetic word to write this book. God placed Deborah in my path to give me a prophetic word that my husband was on the way as well. God allowed me to meet her in a parking lot. When receiving a prophetic word, know God's Spirit and know that it is God.

Introduction

This book was written to help those who are lost and need an encouraging word to step out of your dark tunnels. It was written to help you walk by faith and see the light at the end of your tunnel, realizing that no matter what trials and tribulations you may face, JESUS is the only answer. He gives us hope when everything else fails. If you SEEK HIM, he will pull you through any circumstance or tunnel. It doesn't matter what you see with the natural eye; He will embrace you and give you comfort to endure. These are words of encouragement from my grandmother and grandfather: "Trust Him."

My Mom

She takes care of me,
She makes me happy.
She is always there for me,
Whenever I need her to be.
Moms are special and very kind,
They usually know what's on your mind.
Whenever I am in trouble,
She helps me on the double.
Whenever I am asleep,
She tucks me in without a peep.
She closes the door,
When she knows I am not awake anymore.
She drives the car,
But the school is far.
When I wake up in the morning I see the sun,
I go to school, I have lots of fun.
I come home and get plenty of rest,
I love my Mom, she is the best.

Love,
Tyrell Otaro (age 9)
(God will use the little ones as his vessel.)

Trust in Him

When times get hard, and you're not sure
What to do,
Look to the one most high, he will surely
Carry you through.

If you don't have enough faith, just believe,
It's because of him that we can receive.

Jehovah Jirah our Provider that's one of his names.
Once he fills you, you will never be the same.

He will move mountains small or big,
He already knows our circumstances,
He doesn't have to search or dig.

Who do they say he is? His name is "Jesus."
Especially when friends let you down, and want
You to look to them,
Remember, "Trust Always in Him."

When you need something just knock,
For he is the "Almighty Rock."
"Trust in Him."

Changes

Shocks in life
Sometimes seem beyond
Our hopes and dreams,
Wait patiently
Personal peace will be found
There is one, WHO is GREATER,
And can turn it all around.

There Is Hope for You

At the end of your rope,
Feel like you just can't cope.
"There is always hope."

Don't put your trust in man.
God is the one who will direct your path,
He is the one with the ultimate plan.

All you have to do, my child, "is open your heart."
That is where it all starts.
I will give you peace, love and happiness.
I will give you eternal "LIFE" that will last.

So don't give up, DON'T give in,
"I am your hope," if you just LET ME in.

My Mate

You say you want a mate,
Don't you get tired of meeting the wrong date?
Don't be in such a hurry, and wait.

God has that divine one waiting for you,
God wants you to be patient and to him be true.

He is getting your mate ready and preparing you.
So you don't have to keep going through.

WAIT on him, PRAY for your mate.
This will be your ULTIMATE date.

The Greatest Counselor

Who will you call,
When you stumble and fall,
He is known as the "GREATEST COUNSELOR" of all.
His line is never busy
And you won't get disconnected.
When things seem so insane,
He heals that great pain.
Jesus is the one who will console you,
Better than what any person can do.
His line is never busy
And you won't get disconnected.
When things seem so insane,
He heals that great pain.
Nobody can heal you like Jesus can.
He is "I AM" your Counselor, your Doctor, your Lawyer
Your Best Plan.
You can count on him when you are going through.
And need someone to talk to.
HE IS
Your Greatest Counselor.

Spiraling Down

An individual spiraling
   Downward
      Hidden Memories
         When morning comes people thinking about
            Their past
               And building direction around memories,
                  The pain, the pain
                     Someone thunderous above
                     Stands
                        Waiting to RESCUE you!

Lean on Him

Walk in the light,
Walk in what God has ordained as right.
Be led by him,
Especially when things seem so grim.

He is the ONE who has the power,
He is the one that will deliver you, in your time of need,
No matter what day or hour.

When you are going through the fire,
He is the one that will take you higher.
Don't get discouraged, just begin to give him PRAISE,
In your time of need, that's when he shall bring peace to your day,
He will give you rest,
When you are going through the test.
LEAN ON HIM!!!!!!

Are You Connected?

Have you ever wondered why life seems so difficult?
Maybe it's because you haven't totally given up.
You search high and low looking for something,
Get connected and give God a ring,
For my father he has everything,
Stop searching and seek GOD now.
He'll give you instructions and show you how.
It's time to get connected,
And have a true relationship with him.
ARE YOU CONNECTED?

Miracles

Jesus was able to make the blind man see,
So can you imagine what he can do for you and me?

He turned water into wine,
Surely he can help us when we get in a bind.

Jesus cursed a fig tree,
Can't you see how much power he has over you and me?

Jesus healed a man who could not see or hear,
He even reattached a man's ear.

Jesus is the only one who can make you pure,
Seek him for that miracle cure.

Jesus was able to calm the sea,
So can you imagine what he can do for YOU and me?

Mother

God has really blessed me,
He has allowed you to have much longevity.

I feel so blessed to still have you in my life,
You have taught me much, even how to conquer strife.

Your light has been a lantern for me,
You have been a guide. You let me know "God is and will
Always be."

You have shown me much unconditional love,
Much like the GREAT ONE from above.

You have truly passed the test,
As one of the greatest moms, ever the very best.
And because of you, I feel so very blessed.

God's Fortune

Troubled heart
Seeking greener grass
A voice replied
"I AM NOT OF GREED"
My gift-giving
Is your fortune
AND I AM ALL THAT YOU MAY NEED.

Life

Life has dealt you a hand,
But GOD has a much greater plan.

You were left fatherless and on your own,
Never knowing you had the greatest father of all,
Who would pick you up and love you
When you stumbled and would sometimes fall.

His loving arms open, waiting to embrace you,
Even those who have been taken advantage of, and those
Who have been abused,
You are the ones he wants to greatly use.

God can heal that pain,
And in your life he shall reign.

God is waiting to show you his great love,
He shall make you pure as a dove.

Sure you may have been treated unfair,
Surely my father is one who really cares.

Life has dealt you a hand,
But GOD has a much GREATER PLAN.

God Is Calling You

Don't run, do what God has called you to do,
He only wants to help, and desires the best for you.

Open up your heart first to him,
Let him show you how to win.

He is your victory in times of trials and tribulation,
He allows us to endure circumstances, to give him praise
And follow his expectations.

Answer his call, he wants a better life for you,
Do what he has called you to do.

Give Him Praise

Give Him praise,
Give Him praise.
Worship the Lord when you are struggling through the day.

Lift His name up.
He will fill your cup.

Give Him praise,
Give Him praise.

It's your praise that will see you through the day,
If you have anything to say.

Let praise be on your heart,
Jesus is waiting for you to do your part.

GIVE HIM PRAISE.

Stop Running

You keep trying to escape,
But God is on your heel.
He wants you to surrender,
Your heart, he will heal.

Don't let it be too late,
He has chosen you to be his servant, stop trying to escape.
His calling upon you is great,

Heed to his voice
This will be your ONLY choice.

Listen to his call.
He is the great one who is the answer to all your problems,
No matter how big or small,
So stop trying to stall.

SUBMIT YOURSELF TO HIS AWESOME CALL!!!!

Dreams

We all have high hopes,
Life will help us climb the rope.

Dreams become reality when God is in charge,
He has a direct route, expect your visions to be large.

When you allow him to be first,
You need not thirst.

He has greater plans, and higher heights,
Consult him and be prepared for the flight.

Seek God's direction, no matter how it may seem.
He is prepared to show you his greatest dream.

The Gift

The gift is eternal life,
God gave us this gift of salvation.
He sent his son, who died on the cross
Just for us.
Do you know a man who would send his son,
To give you life,
To help you with your spiritual flight?
Who wouldn't want to serve him,
One who aids us when life seems so grim.
MY, MY, MY,
THE GIFT, THE GIFT, THE GIFT.

Take Your Place

I called you to run this race,
But as life would have it, you want to operate in another place.

My anointing will not be upon you,
Until you do what I have called you to do.

My power is in you, my message you will bring,
This is when you will feel my great anointing.

I will give you favor and grace,
When you take your place.

God's Promise

Seek my kingdom first,
And have a great thirst.

I have abundant life just for you,
I need you to get close to me.
That's all you need to do.

I have your life already planned,
Just take my hand.

I have a covenant with you,
Follow my lead,
And you won't miss my promise indeed.

Double-minded

Will you serve me,
Or will you serve the enemy?

You must make a choice,
If you want life, you will choose my voice.

You can't serve two masters,
This would be your greatest disaster.

You can't continue to straddle,
Sooner or later you will feel the battle.

Choose the one you will serve,
The one you choose is the one you chose to observe.

You must make a choice,
If you want life, you will choose MY voice.

Prayer Time

Do you spend any time with me?
How can you grow spiritually?

How can you get to know me?
Come to me with your requests,
I'll help you make it through your tests.

You must spend time communicating with me,
My glory you shall see,

Come, Come, Come
And share some time with me,
My glory, my glory
You shall see!!!!!

The Good Book

You must read my Word daily,
My Word is what will strengthen you,
Read, Read, Read,
That's all you have to do.

My Word is your instruction manual,
Surely this you can handle.

My Word will help you understand correction,
And give you great direction.

My Word brings knowledge and wisdom.
This you must read and live to reach my kingdom.

This is how you get hooked,
Read my Word daily, this is the good book.

I Spared You

You came close to losing your life,
Through all the turmoil and strife.
There is a reason I spared you,
I have something awesome for you to do.
It's not often you get a second chance,
So take this as an opportunity in advance.
Give your life to me, while you may,
This will be your most "GLORIOUS DAY."

It's Your Season

God's blessings are many if we faithfully serve him.
He has many abundant gifts for us,
God wants us to put in him our trust.

All he needs is a reason,
To bless us in our season.

If you have been faithful and stayed on course,
He will bless you; he's your source.

Your blessings won't always be money,
He has many reasons to make your day sunny.

He will give you favor and grace,
You will have security with him in that secret place.

God just wants a reason,
TO BLESS YOU IN DUE SEASON!!!!!!!!!!!!!!

Mountain, You Must Move

We go through life,
Experiencing ups and downs and strife,

Our circumstances make our mountains seem so great,
If you pray and praise God,
That mountain he will eliminate.

We have to speak to that mountain,
God can move this, his word is our fountain.

Drink from his Word, and command that mountain to move,
His Word works, that he will prove.

MOUNTAIN, YOU MUST MOVE!!

Is There a Void?

So you feel like something is missing in your life,
You keep looking for that husband, that wife.

You try to replace that void with alcohol and drugs,
I am the one you need, who can embrace you supernaturally
With hugs.

Stop trying to find happiness in other things,
Search for me and see what life brings.

I honor those who get close to me,
I bring about change, be a branch on my tree.

I will fill that space,
If you seek "MY FACE."

Been Abused

People have mistreated you,
Made you feel so low you didn't know what to do.

Surely you've been abused
And certainly misused.

I want to use you for my glory,
Within your life there is a story.

You see your life will be a test-i-mony for others to see,
Don't run, don't flee.

Come only to me.
Surely you may feel weak,
I am the one you need to seek.

I can make your life better than you can imagine it would be,
Come only to me.

Is Your Life Scrambled (from Drugs)?

Is your life in shambles?
You feel so scrambled.

Wondering how did I reach this point,
You took a wrong turn and ended up at this joint.

After a while he knew you by name,
He started calling you daily to play his game.

You forgot about everybody and everything,
You even stole from others every time he gave you a ring.

I sent my son to deliver you,
This is what my father sent me to do.

You can be healed instantly, just cry out to me,
I can change your life.

It will be different, you will see,
Open up your mouth and cry out to me.

Healing

I can heal your body if you have faith in me,
Sometimes the doctors give you up and tell
You how it's going to be.

Those who don't have faith or know of me,
Become hopeless and accept what they see.

Become strong in me, and become bold,
I have the last word.

I am the "GREAT HEALER," I hold the "KEY,"
All you have to do is believe in me.

And when the doctors tell you "Oh no,"
Remember I have the "Last Word."

I am the "GREAT HEALER," I hold the "KEY,"
All you have to do is believe in me.

The Homeless One

Many people overlook you,
Some even turn their noses up too.

You may be an angel that I have sent,
They may even find you under a tent.

So be kind to those on the street,
You may never know, whom you will greet.

I will take the lowest and make a great man
Or woman of God,
So think twice before you look at them so odd.

You may never know, whom you will meet,
So "BE KIND TO THOSE ON THE STREETS."

Humble Yourself

I can't use you if you're all puffed up,
Already filled is your cup.

I need a vessel that I can mold,
One that will honor me, and for me be bold.

One who has my spirit, and I am moving within you,
Not one who boasts of themselves and what
They can do.

I elevate the humble and the meek,
Those are the chosen I use to speak.

People will see my glory upon you,
"Great Things" shall I do.

Divorce

Parents are getting a divorce.
The children suffer too,
Everything is off course.

Parents get mad,
Children become sad.

If you took the time to pray,
I could give you answers to help
You along the way.

Hearts to mend with such great pain,
Seek me, you have much to gain.

When all else fails,
I'm the one who sets the sail.

Divorce is painful, and you suffer great pain,
Turn to me, there is so much to gain.

Depression

There is an enemy who troubles your mind,
He takes you in all directions, puts your emotions in a bind.

He tangles your mind like tying a rope,
He tries so hard to make you give up hope.

He makes you feel like you're all alone
In a tunnel in the dark,
But know this, there is one greater, who will leave
His mark.

I will cleanse your mind and your heart,
Just let me open that door, to a new start.

Take the time to get to know me,
"YOUR MIND I WILL SET FREE."

Forgive

You have carried around with you for so many years,
Oh the hurt, the pain, and the tears.

The pain has even broken up homes,
Some have left this earth feeling all alone.

You say you know me but you don't forgive,
Remember my Word says you must do so
In order to live.

You are to be an imitation of me,
You must represent me as an example for others to see,

So don't let anger take control,
This will stop the blessings that I hold,

In order to live,
"YOU MUST FORGIVE."

Because of You

When I was small,
Many names I was called.

They said I would never amount to anything,
But to you I am a "King."

People judged me and said what I could not do,
I knew I had a father who would carry me through.

They said I would be a nobody,
But in Christ "I AM SOMEBODY."

Because of you, I can achieve the mission
You set for me,
Those words people have spoken "WILL
NOT BE."

I will be an OVERCOMER because of THEE.

Thirst for Me

Drink of my cup
Instead of the alcohol you sup.

I know you have trouble,
Sometimes you feel like you are stuck
In a puddle.

I know you feel pain,
I can remove that stain.

No one knows what you go through,
I know all, and know it is not easy for you.

Surrender your life to me,
Oh you will see,
Life can be better if you "THIRST for ME."

Are You Prepared?

If I came in the middle of the night,
Would you be prepared and is your
Heart right?

You won't know when I may decide to come back,
So prepare your house and let nothing be lack.

The time is short and also very near,
Be sure everything is clear.

Don't think because you are young you have
Plenty of time,
I may come like the drop of a dime.

Surely you must know that I truly care,
So get your house in order and be prepared.

Witness

How can you be so selfish with my love?
I am the one who healed you, "The Great
One from Above."

There are others out there who are also lost,
Some have already paid a price and at all cost.

I expect you to help others find their way,
Remember, I did not allow you to go astray.

Go, tell many how much I care,
My son gave his life, so your life
Would be spared.

Tell them, tell them,
"HOW MUCH I CARE."

Losing Someone Special

You lost a loved one, no one can take
Their place,
"JESUS" can fill that empty space.

I know it is difficult trying to find your way,
Come to me, in your heart I will stay.

Come let me embrace you,
That's what I will do.

I want to show you I can heal that pain,
So you can go on with your life and not
Feel so drained.

Bring your burdens to me,
I want to heal you, this you shall see.

Come my son, my daughter,
Come only to me,
Life will be better,
This you SHALL see.

The Brokenhearted

I know you have been wounded, and I feel your pain,
I know you feel like life is not worth living again.

Let me tell you a story,
I am waiting to show you my glory.

I know you have been bruised and built up walls.
When my Spirit is not in you, you are bound to fall.

No man, no woman, can heal your heart.
Come to me, I'll bring you out of the dark.

I am the only one, who has that healing power,
Come to me with your needs this hour.

I know you have been wounded and I feel your pain,
I will give you life once again.

God Is

God Is . . . Peace in the midst of a storm,
God Is . . . There when you have no money in your account.
God Is . . . Your way-maker when you see no way,
God Is . . . Your help when you are having problems on the job.
God Is . . . Your counselor when you are having problems in
Your marriage,
God Is . . . Your helpmate when your mate walks out on you.
God Is . . . There when children act out.
God Is . . . Your help when a loved one is on drugs,
God Is . . . There when you lose a loved one.
God Is . . . There when you have given up on life,
God Is . . . Your deliverer in your time of need.
God Is . . . Peace in the midst of a storm,
GOD IS . . .

Who Is the Judge?

No one is without fault,
So be careful how you talk.

I know people have a tendency to tell you how
They feel,
But be careful of the words you spill.

It's only within my power,
I am the judge of the hour.

Be careful how critical you may be,
How you judge someone else may come back to thee.

The Tongue

That sharp-edged sword,
Which sometimes causes great discord.

Our words have power,
Be careful of the words you speak this hour.
Your words move in the atmosphere,
They can cause great pain and shed many tears.

If you are one who likes to carry a story,
Be sure it will edify me, and give me glory.

Remember you can create a mess,
Or you can use your words for others to be blessed.

This Is a Test

Have you been going through,
Experiencing difficulty and feeling confused,
And don't know what to do?

I am tearing down the old,
And rebuilding the new.

You will never, never be the same.
I am rebuilding and reshaping,
Taking you on a higher plane.
You must go through this test,
I am molding you to be at your best.

So "accept the challenge and go through the test."

Who Is Your God?

Is it your home you consider your throne?
Is it your honey, or could it possibly be your money?

Is it your vehicle you polish every day?
Or is it your wardrobe you like to display?
Surely this is not God's plan,
Nor will it continue to stand.

God is not pleased if he is not first,
Surely your world could very well burst.

"Who is your God?"

The Dating Game

And oh what a game,
You meet this one, then another one,
After a while they all seem the same.

You meet someone who seems like they have it all together,
After one or two dates they are as flaky as the weather.

You'll meet a married woman or a married man,
Then you find out, oh no, this is not the right plan.

Stop searching, I am the one you need to seek
Come to me first, I'll give you a mate for keeps.

Going through the Fire

Don't doubt me, I will never let you down,
You follow my path, you are surely heaven bound.

Shadrach, Meschach, and Abednego went through the fire,
They never gave up, nor did they lose their desire

To follow me,
Because of their faith, they could see.

They believed I would come to their rescue,
Don't doubt me, I will do the same for you.

Go through the fire, and know I am there,
Your pain and hurt, I will surely bear.

And "I WILL WALK WITH YOU," so don't be scared.

Pass Over

All of your promotions come from me,
So don't worry if they pass over thee.

Just seek my face,
I have the control of where you are placed.

Stop trying to do it on your own,
I have it mapped out for you, even
Before you were born.

Many of you do what you do to move higher,
Remember I am your supplier.

So don't worry if you have been passed over,
But of course,
I am your source.

Temptation

Don't be fooled by the enemy's tools;
He's out to get you to join his school.

He's out to hinder your blessings,
And destroy what God has destined.

To those who are married, he'll plant someone
Else in your path,

It may look good, but you will soon feel the enemy's wrath,

He likes to tempt you to get you off track,
Don't let him climb on your back.

The enemy will always bring you temptation,
Remember your commitment and dedication.

He's trying to take you down another road,
Don't be his foolish toad.

Look before you leap,
Your soul I shall keep.

Recognize the enemy before it's too late,
Send that enemy running with his bait.

Spiritual Growth

Remember you started out from dust, almost like a weed,
Then I planted my spirit to germinate your seed.
The more you read my Word

You will feel the sprinkle of my spirit that I sow,
The more you read, I will water you to grow.

Once the Word is in you, you must obey my laws,
The Holy Spirit will keep you from the enemy's flaws.

You will grow from a root to a strong tree,
You will grow up and be what I cultivated you to be
As long as you allow me to water your tree.

You Won't Hear

I have been calling you,
And have given you many warnings too.

I put angels in your path to tell you about me,
But you keep ignoring me and you won't see.

Open your eyes, and take heed to my call,
You won't have many more chances.
So don't continue to stall.

This could be the last time my angels come near.
So surrender your life, be obedient and hear.

I Am Trying to Reach You

I sent my messenger to call you by phone,
But your friend told my messenger you
Were not at home.

I sent my messenger to call you by cell,
You said, "I don't want what you are trying to sell."

I sent my messenger to contact you by pager,
You phoned back and said, "Oh this is nothing major."

I sent my messenger to contact you by e-mail,
You said, "I don't have time, I plan to sail."

I sent my messenger, so don't ignore my call,
It may be your last chance,
So please don't stall.

Tell Your Story

How can you share my glory,
If you don't know my story?

You wonder why I am so blessed,
You don't know the trials, nor the tests.

I have a story that needs to be told,
The situations I've been through,
Oh, what the future holds.

Most people would not believe what
I have endured,
Only my father knows what I have explored.

You may have to travel many, many miles,
And experience many, many trials.

So tell your story,
God will get the glory.

You Say You Come in My Name

You say you come in my name,
But your actions bring me shame,
Your mouth, you need to tame.

You must walk in your new nature,
I made you a new creature.

If you are walking with me,
You have to walk upright for others to see.

You can't come to me halfway,
The door to heaven will not be opened
To you today.

So if you say you come in my name,
Please don't bring me any shame.

Don't Move till I Tell You

There are times when you want to step
Out on your own,
But when you do, you will be all alone.

If you have my Spirit in you,
You will move when I tell you to
And you will do only what I say do.

But when you step out on your own will,
My plans for you will stand still.

If you move by my timing,
You will continue to keep climbing.

Only move when I tell you to,
My Spirit will give you guidance on what to do.

Wounded

So you have been wounded along the way,
In someone's church, you chose not to stay.

I know you are in pain,
And chose not to return again.

Don't go back out in the world,
The enemy will raise havoc, and take you for a twirl.

Seek my face and get in my presence,
I will lead you, this is of essence.

Don't let this pain,
Allow the enemy to reign.

Come to me, I'll heal that wound,
Don't get caught in darkness and gloom.
Open your heart and for me make room.

Forget Your Past

You don't have to worry about your past,
I sent my son who paid the price,
So you would have eternal life,
That will always last.

I washed away all your sins,
Only you and I know where you have been.

Before I can move you to the next level,
You must say, "Get behind me, devil."

You don't have to fear what you have done,
I placed my Spirit inside of you,
The battle is already won.

Put the past behind you, and leave it there,
My concern for you is my greatest care.

Adversity

When adversity comes knocking at your door,
Will you run and hide, or seek the Lord?

God's Word will assist you,
If you do what it instructs you to do.

It's the Word that comforts you in times of trouble,
Don't let the enemy burst your bubble.

Have faith in the great one above,
He cares for you, and wants to embrace you with His love.

So pray, read the word, and PRAISE God
When those hard times come,
Don't let the enemy cause you to run!!!!!!!!!!

Seek Me

When drugs and alcohol call your name,
Seek me, "JESUS," I'll recharge you again.

Those substances can't do what I do,
What you consider a high is only temporary for you.

You can't run when you are in distress,
Seek me, I'll give you rest.

Those problems will leave you for a little while,
They will still be there sitting in your mind on file.

Come to me,
I'll set you free,

Those substances can't do what I can do.

Remember, just call on me,
I'll recharge you and set you free,
"Look only to me."

Now You Can Fly

From a cocoon to a beautiful butterfly,
You started out as a cocoon, now it's time to fly.

The Word is inside of you,
You must tell others of my love,
So they will know of the "Great
One" from above.

So many are lost, and don't have a clue,
You must go out and witness too.

So many are hungry, and are waiting on you.
"Speak my Word," that is what you will do.

You started out as a "Cocoon,"
Now it's time to "Fly."

I Wrote the Manuscript

You keep trying to plan your life,
Looking for that husband, that wife.

The script is already planned for you,
Follow my lead, is all you need to do.

Stop trying to do it on your own,
Lean on me and the story will unfold.
It's already in your design. This I know.

So "Stop trying to help me,
Just follow the script."

If the Head Is Bad, the Body Is Dead

If the leader doesn't properly lead his sheep,
How can I expect souls to be saved for keeps?

I look to you to walk upright,
Your sheep follow what they see by sight.

I hold you accountable for what they see,
So walk upright so my sheep don't flee.

You are accountable for their souls,
So represent me well, be strong and be bold.

My sheep are looking up to you,
So many souls will make it through.

This is the job I have left for you,
So lead my sheep, so they make it through.

I Brought You Out, Don't Go Back

The enemy keeps trying to persuade you to go
Back into the world,
So he can take you on another whirl.

I brought you out so your life would be changed,
So life would not seem so deranged.

The enemy tries to make you feel like you're missing something,
All he wants is your company.

So think twice before you decide to drift,
And let him take you on that cliff.

The enemy will cause you strife,
Remember I gave you life.

I Stand at the Door

I stand at the door,
With open arms waiting to embrace you,
And show you what to do.

Walk through the door,
I have a new life,
And so much more.

Stop trying to decide if you should
Come through,
I hold my hand out waiting for you.

So walk through the door to new beginnings,
Say goodbye to the life you were not winning.

For you I have so much more,
I stand at the door.

The Battle

So being saved seems so hard,
You must always keep your guard.

God will keep you, if you want to be kept,
He hears your cry, when you have wept.

He wants you to cry out to him,
Especially when the battle seems so grim.

"I control the earth and the wind,
So when you need me, I'll step in."

"I control every trial you face,
Come to me, I'll give you grace."

Generational Curses

So you've experienced many things in your life,
It's the curse that is causing you strife.

Depression, abuse, medical problems, drugs and alcohol,
There are many.
You don't have to accept these curses,
God's Spirit can break every generational curse.
His great Spirit is plenty.

So pray and bind up those forces which try
To betray you.
You don't have to be trapped,
God has a great life for you already mapped.

So tell those curses to bow the knee,
Say, "I will be all that GOD wants me to be."

Man Pleasers

"I am not looking for those who want
To be exalted by man,
If we exalt you, there's no room for my plan."

"I created the earth,
There is no other like me,
I didn't choose man to have people worship thee."

"I chose you as an example to carry
Out my requests,
Even you shall experience some tests."

"So don't look for those to exalt you,
I am greater than you,
You can't do what I do."

Angels

I send my angels to watch over you,
Yes, that is what I do.

My angels have wings you can't see,
They are there to help thee.

My angels come to comfort you,
Yes, that is what I send them to do.

My angels come when your cabinets are bare,
I send them because I care.

My angels are there when you run out of gas,
All you have to do is ask,
You know my voice; your cares, you may cast.

I send my angels to watch over you,
Yes, that is what I do.

You Can't Exhale, if You Don't Inhale

If you don't take anything in,
How can you expect to win?

Read and eat my Word every day,
Sleep my word when you lay.

You must gravitate to my Spirit,
Every day you must live it.

Just like attending school,
If you don't study, you don't rule.

If you don't take anything in,
How can you expect to win?

Search for Me

"I AM THE KEY."
You have looked for many things to make
You feel good,
But what I have never understood.

Why you didn't seek me,
But as life would be.

You search sometimes until eternity,
"I AM THE KEY."

You need not search any longer,
Come to me "I'LL MAKE YOU STRONGER."

Stop looking to people and other things,
Seek me "I'll give you new wings."

SEARCH FOR ME
"I AM THE KEY."

Walkie-talkie for GOD

Speak my WORD only,
Even when it may feel lonely.

Speak my WORD,
Many do not hear, and many have not heard,
Speak my WORD.

I don't need eloquent words,
I want everyone to understand what they have heard.

I want people to understand my laws,
So they can live without flaws.

So speak my WORD, and be very bold,
You have words that need to be told.

Stay on Track, Don't Go Back

The enemy is trying to persuade you to turn back,
Remember what life was like, and what you lacked.

You had no peace, and you had no joy,
The enemy will grab you, and treat you like a toy.
Your life he will try to destroy.

I'll give you life filled with my Spirit,
When the enemy comes, don't hear it.

He will take you on a trip,
Your life he will sift.

The enemy will bring back turmoil and confusion,
Your mind you will be losing,
So stay on track don't go back.

God's Plan

My plan for you,
Is different than what you would do.

I have a plan designed especially for you,
You have no idea where I am taking you.
So stay focused, that's what you need to do.

Stop trying to do it on your own,
I am taking you on a HIGHER ZONE.

Don't let anyone change your course,
Or you will be led by another force.

Come with me and let me show you the way,
With me you need to stay.

So follow me and take my hand,
And you shall see my "great plan."

Quiet Time

Come and spend some quiet time with me,
Get by yourself is where you need to be.

Sit down and be quiet, so I can talk to you,
Then you will know what I want you to do.

You need quiet time so I can speak,
Search for me and I will take you deep.

It's in your quiet time I will convey thoughts to you,
So you will know what I want you to do.

So find that special place,
So you can listen to me daily in our own secret space.

Your Mission

You are on a mission, so keep the charge,
Even when things seem so difficult, and
may even seem hard.

Circumstances will come and try to get in your way,
You tell those mountains to move, God is moving today,
I am carrying a torch on this Jesus-filled day.

You keep passing the baton, and run the race,
Know that God has set for you a special place.

So do what God tells you and take your position,
He sent you to carry out his great mission.

Broken Up and Broken Down

Someone has left you with a broken heart,
Seek me, I'll give you a new start.

Only you and I know the pain you are going through,
If you come to me I'll mend you like new.

I see your heart, and I see your pain,
I want to heal you and remove that stain.

Don't seek others to heal your heart,
They may also pick you apart.

Come only to me,
And I will set you free.

Only I can heal that pain,
And make you like new again.

Half-baked Christian

So you want to live on both sides of the fence,
And you wonder why your life seems so dense.

This life you must choose,
Or your life you will lose.

You can't live life any kind of way,
You must serve me, my laws you must obey.

If you are doing things you know won't please me,
Search yourself and ask would thou be
Pleased with thee.

You can't go out and live like the world,
The enemy will put you in his web, and take
You for a twirl.

So choose whom you will serve,
The life you choose is the one you deserve.

A Date with Jesus

I have a date with Jesus, and I can't be late,
I must be on time to meet with him.

I can't be late,
This is a very special date.

This date will cause my life to change,
In him my life will be rearranged.

This will be the best date ever,
My life will experience new levels.

I have a date with Jesus, and I can't be late,
This will be a very "special date."

Drink from the Well

Your life will excel,
Drink from the well.

Thirst for me,
And you shall see.

I have plenty for you to drink,
My well overflows for you,
Life will be better than you think.
Drink from the well.

I'll fill your cup too,
This is what I will do.

DRINK, DRINK, DRINK.

I Reign

No matter what you go through, I "reign,"

No matter what storm comes your way, I "reign."

No matter how bad it looks, "I reign."

When you lose your job, "I reign."

When your wife or husband walks out on you, "I reign,"

When you don't have enough money to
Pay your bills, "I reign."

When you are left taking care of the children, "I reign,"

When your car is repossessed, "I reign."

When people talk about you, "I reign,"

Lay before me and speak your needs.

Then "PRAISE ME" for it, and "GIVE
THANKS, PLEASE."

Broken

So you are broken and all worn down,
And wondering what caused you to be bound.

You keep asking how did I get in this mess?
What you did not know, "I can give you rest."

When you are so far down and can't see your way out,
"Cry out to me and I will give you a new route."

Yes, life can have its ups and downs,
You can be on an emotional roller coaster,
And go through many rounds.

When you have reached this point,
And feel like you don't know what to do,
"MY ARMS ARE OPEN JUST WAITING
ON YOU."

Blessings

I am so glad God sent you to me,
I had no idea how this would be.
When you serve God, he brings things to thee.

You must put God first in your life,
God will send you that husband, that wife.

Serve him with all your heart,
That's where it all starts.

I am glad he had a divine plan,
And he placed you in my hand.

(This poem is dedicated to my husband. My husband was sent
to me from a prophetic word from God after I prayed and
waited on God.)

Abusing the Gifts

You have been anointed with special gifts,
"No don't let the enemy make you drift."

I gave you those gifts, to use for my mission,
Don't let the enemy change your position.

If you lead people astray,
With your life you shall pay.

If you don't use your gifts for my glory,
There's no need for you to tell your story.

Graveyard Gifts

I gave you gifts and here you sit,
You let those gifts lie in a pit.

You come to church for years and sit on a pew,
"Yes, that is what you do."

I gave you gifts for you to move when I tell you to,
Not to keep your gifts dormant inside of you.

Life passed you by, your gifts you did not use,
Now your life is over, and you are through.

"YOUR GIFTS WENT TO THE GRAVE WITH YOU."

A New Life with Thee

Father, I give my life to you,
Please tell me what to do.

I need a change in my life,
I am tired of so much strife.

Guide me, Lord, into your world,
I am through letting the enemy take
Me for a twirl.

If you let the enemy take control,
He will suddenly have a stronghold.

I need a change in my life,
I am tired of so much strife.

FATHER, I GIVE MY LIFE TO THEE.

(REPEAT ROMANS 10:9-10)

About the Author

Annette Hoggs-Jackson enjoys expressing words through poetry, a gift to her from God. Annette enjoys reading, writing, sewing, decorating, and encouraging women, young people, and anyone who needs help. She also enjoys motivational speaking. Her poetry has been published in an anthology. Annette is a graduate of San Jose University in San Jose, California, where she earned a degree in psychology. She has worked with people with mental health issues, including juvenile delinquents, young men and women, the elderly, and families. Annette is currently working with families, the homeless, the abused, and the divorced, with problems such as domestic abuse, drug and alcohol addiction, depression, and schizophrenia. Annette and her husband are in the ministry together. Their organization is called Christians Merging Together (CMT). Annette resides in Daytona Beach, Florida, with her husband, Sammy, her son Tyrell, and stepson, Samuel Jackson.

Author Contact Information

Annette Hoggs-Jackson

P.O. Box 10782

Daytona Beach, Florida 32120

E-mail: Sammy050657@aol.com

www.ingramcontent.com/pod-product-compliance
Lightning Source LLC
Chambersburg PA
CBHW032013040426

42448CB00006B/619